Working The Net:
A Practical Guide to Business Networking

By Simon Bozeat

Written by Simon Bozeat

http://www.simonbozeat.com

Compiled, Edited and Published by GD Publishing

Other Books by GD Publishing

Making It Rain by Simon Bozeat

http://bit.ly/makingitrain

21st Century Tactics by Glyn Williams

http://bit.ly/21stcenturytactics

The 7 Deadly Sins of Advertising By Glyn Williams

http://bit.ly/7-deadly

The Holy Grail Trading System By James Windsor

http://bit.ly/grailtrading

Watch six free videos from simon's course

"How to Build a Profitable Business Network"

At www.simonbozeat.com

And

Read Simon's Blog for more networking articles

Table of Contents

Introduction

Hello and welcome to 'Working The Net' a business book for people who want to learn how to network effectively in order to rub shoulders with the people they want to do business with.

First off, let me state that true business networking is NOT just about going to endless business clubs and mixing with people that half the time have no bearing on your business at all. There are literally thousands of networking events held in every country of the world and many people believe that networking is about meandering aimlessly from one business club to the next. That is NOT real business networking.

Many of our clients have asked us to put together this course as a quick and easy-to-read guide to real business networking principles

The book is based on a training course I first ran in 2003 to clients in professional services such as accountancy and law. They wanted to learn how to transform contacts into relationships and relationships into profitable business. As we all know the world has changed massively since then. Now, more than ever, it is crucial to build high quality relationships with clients and the people who can refer you to your next major sale.

Each Chapter comprising stories, how-to's, how-not-to's, techniques and some secrets of people who have built exceptional networks of talented, influential and powerful people on their way to the top of their chosen profession.

Together they form a mini-course that unfolds over the coming pages.

At the end of the book you will learn about the exciting and informative training events and coaching services that we can deliver for you. All of our services related to coaching and teaching people how to increase their wealth have a unique guarantee… either they deliver or we keep working with you for free until they do!

Finally before we begin to look at how to become an effective Networker I'd like to introduce you to the most important part of this book.

Having been on literally hundreds of training seminars and delivered tens of thousands of training hours I know one thing about people and their ability to follow through on good intentions, most people don't!. Many learn a lot but they don't put into practice what they've been taught even though at the time it makes great sense.

For example, one guy I worked with at a Telecoms multi-national some years ago went on enough training courses to make him president of the world! Yet he never moved past the role of Chief Accountant. Why? Because there was one ingredient lacking; application. Learning is one thing and doing is another.

By the way I have nothing against accountants!

A smart person once said… "Everyone wants to be successful but not everyone wants to practice"

Everything you will read within these pages is the product of thousands of hours research through observation, personal experience and reading many books/articles and listening to tapes. I've done all the hard work and learned about all the mistakes people make so you don't have to.

Having said all of this it is worth highlighting a common fallacy, it goes like this…

 "Those that take action get results"

Now I believe any idiot can *'take action'*. It's the people that take action doing the stuff that works that get results! There's a big difference.

One of my favourite analogies I've used for many years on coaching workshops is this:

Imagine if today Tiger Woods was being trained to play golf. His tutor or coach might look for just the slightest change to his swing, grip, stance, tactics or mental toughness to gain a 0.005% improvement in his game.

Now think of me learning how to play golf. The most I've ever done is 9 holes on a 'Pitch & Putt' course by the seaside. For me to learn the game it would require a complete root and branch approach.

Since writing this I have received a great deal of feedback either unsolicited or requested directly by my team. It has reaffirmed what I suspected, that there is something in this book for everyone irrespective of your level of experience and competence.

So whether you are a Tiger Woods or a Simon Bozeat of golf or somewhere in between you will find things in this book that will either be very new or a simple reinforcement & reminder of what you already know.

I look forward to learning what they are.

About The Book

Let's make a start, a short story…

'From Pride Park to the Royal Albert Hall'

On Wednesday 30th April 2003 I had the privilege of attending the 100th Centenary Convention of the Institute of Directors (IoD). This was held at the Royal Albert Hall in London. The speakers included Sir Richard Branson, Lady Thatcher, Sir Stephen Redgrave and Buzz Aldrin plus many other distinguished people from the world of commerce.

An exceptional line up of speakers by anyone's standards. Naturally it attracted many leading business leaders. Before, during and after the day I had the opportunity to rub shoulders with some highly influential people and secured some valuable business leads.

Since then I was invited to be a guest speaker at a prestigious networking group in my local area comprising senior figures from many of the professional services companies who are on my target list to do business with.

As I result of the seminar and subsequent conversations I was recently invited to interview the partners in one of the most profitable law firms in the UK. This is part of an extensive research study into understanding the factors that both contribute to and hinder sales success in professional service firms. The research will be a springboard to the delivery of a suite of training and coaching activities that took my business to the next level of success.

The sponsor, himself an accomplished networker, is providing me with a continuous stream of names of highly influential people all of which are more than happy to see me. All I do is ask him if he knows a decision maker in one of my target companies. Invariably he does and contact is made. This makes selling so much easier!

You might be asking what the point of this story is. Simply, it is a graphic illustration of the power of effective networking, or as I call it the result of 'Working the Net.'

The reason I was there was the result of meeting with Kevin, another Consultant in my field, some 12 months prior at a formal networking event held at the Pride Park Conference Centre in Derby (Home of Derby County Football Club).

 Cutting a long story short, Kevin became a member of a networking group of Business Coaches I ran for a short while in the Midlands. After a few meetings he mentioned he was a member of the IoD and suggested we make a pitch to deliver some seminars for the Institute. This we did and presumably because our workshop was particularly well received one participant invited me as a guest to the IoD Convention.

This story is not in any way meant to impress you but to impress upon you the importance of approaching networking with planning and purpose. Many, but certainly not all, of the steps in the journey from Pride Park to the Royal Albert Hall were calculated to get me to meet people with power and influence and it will serve as another step to mix with the great and good.

It is worth mentioning that the invitation to the convention was an unexpected and delightful surprise and indeed not all the steps went exactly to plan. That's the beauty of effective networking; no matter how well you plan your campaign always expect the unexpected.

We have spent over seven years researching what effective networkers do. This has involved attending over 200 formal and informal networking events and countless hours following up leads and contacts. Not only did we use these to further my own business but also to research what differentiates the top networkers from the average.

You will be glad to know there are many actions that top networkers take that are simply common sense and there are many, many mistakes that you should be aware of. However, the good news is that I'm going to tell you what these mistakes are so you can avoid making them! Also I will include some secrets from the best of the best networkers I have researched.

This is what we will cover in this book

Part 1 - Five Common Mistakes

This will cover why networking is so important and why it is an essential part of creating the conditions whereby your business is promoted through positive-word-of- mouth-advertising. I'll open your mind to the biggest mistakes that inexperienced networkers make time and time again

Part 2 - Three Things You MUST Do

If you are going to be an effective networker then here are three things you must do first

This chapter also gives you a quick self-assessment diagnostic to help you assess where you are in relation to your networking activities.

Part 3 - Three Ways to Motivate Advocates

This covers just three ways you can motivate people to become your advocates and help you rub shoulders with the people you want to do business with.

Part 4 Preparing For a Networking Event

This part covers three things you should do before attending any networking event.

Part 5 Working a Room

Covering just five skills and techniques for making the most of a formal or informal networking event.

Part 6 How to Strike Up a Conversation

Exactly how do you start talking to someone that you've never met?

Part 7 - Your Three Types of Network

This covers the idea of 'designing the perfect network before you need it.' It includes the three types of network you need to be successful.

- Support Network
- Information Network
- Referral Network

Part 8 - Knowing Your Network

This gives you just one of the many networking planning tools introduced to participants and subscribers to the *'How to Build a Profitable Business Network'* online and live training programme. This tool covers where to go to obtain sources of support.

It also includes a quick quiz which demonstrates how little people generally know about the people in their network.

Part 9 Becoming a Revenue Enhancer

This part introduces the concept of a 'revenue enhancer' and a five step process for earning more revenue for your customers and you in the process.

Part 10 Are You Listening?

The importance of the most important communication skill of all yet, for many, the most difficult to master; listening.

Part 11 - Summary

This is full review of the entire book plus where to go to obtain some further top networking tips

What's in it for you?

I have yet to come across anyone who has been successful in business without building solid relationships with a wide network of influential and talented people. Talk to any leading business figure about how they got to the top and they will name people that have helped them get there.

The people in their network have been both sources of great advice and influential advocates of the individual and their organisation plus the products or services they represent.

Anyone who sells anything will tell you the most powerful and cheapest form of advertising is word-of-mouth. Great networkers have the ability to build an extension of their sales team. Just imagine how good life will be when you have an ever increasing population of colleagues who almost feel duty bound to exalt the virtues of you to the people they meet.

I guarantee that if you choose to learn and act on the principles outlined in this book you will improve your ability to network and therefore earn fatter commission cheques!

Five Common Mistakes

As discussed earlier I am going to highlight the five most common mistakes made by inexperienced networkers…

- Spending too much time with people who are not in a position to help
- Only focussing on what *you* want
- Not keeping in touch
- Not believing in what you have to sell
- Thinking that 'working the net' means just going to networking events

Let's look at them one by one.

1.   Spending too much time with people who are not in a position to help

Some years ago I was involved with a business referral organisation. It asks its members to meet once a week for a couple of hours in the morning to learn about each other's businesses. Members, in-between meetings, are then encouraged to refer business to each other. This leads to a healthy exchange of hot leads which often translates into excellent business.

In my view it is an excellent organisation with a tried and tested format that for many members works extremely well.

Unfortunately for me there were far too few people in my particular group who regularly came into contact with the sort of person who were likely to be interested in the services I was promoting at the time.

As a friend pointed out 'Simon, I can't see you getting too many leads from Boo-Boo the Clown!'

A big mistake that many people make is to spend too much time with people who may have the greatest of intentions and be very interested in you and what you have to offer. However if they are not in a position to do business with or refer you they can consume too much of your time and lead you nowhere.

2.   Only focusing on what *you* want

If your profession involves selling products and/or services you will know how important it is to learn about the features and benefits of what it is you have to sell. You will practice many of the sales skills; qualifying, presenting, negotiating, closing etc. All good practice and essential if you want to be successful.

However, networking is a two way street, it is not just about you, it is about what others want.

Therefore the second biggest mistake people make is to only focus on what you want to sell and how useful people are in helping you get what you want. This can be seen as rude, arrogant and entirely counter -productive. If played to the extreme this behavior pushes people away rather than endearing them to you.

17

3.   Not keeping in touch

As you will see in later chapters the quality of your network relies on the quality of relationships you build with people. I have witnessed hundreds of networkers who fail to keep in touch with potentially extremely influential advocates.

In one case I needed some work done on my computer. An expert happened to catch me one day and I invited him in to work on my system. In one afternoon he did an excellent job. That was 26 months ago & I haven't heard anything from him since! A shame, because I'd be more than happy to refer him to others.

There are a host of reasons why people don't keep in touch ranging from simply forgetting, not being organised or even not thinking the person is worthwhile keeping in touch with. I've even had people tell me they don't know how to keep in touch!

4.   Not believing in what you have to sell

This is blindingly obvious but perhaps is the number one reason why many salespeople do not succeed. Not even the most accomplished actor can consistently get away with selling something they fundamentally don't believe in.

We could go on and spend many hundreds of pages talking about the importance of belief and attitude. There simply isn't sufficient space to do so and it would detract from the main purpose of this book. However, to reinforce, if you don't believe in what you are selling don't expect others to!

5.   Thinking that 'Networking For Business' means just going to networking events

I've often heard people talk about formal networking events as if they are the be all and end all of networking. I've been to dozens and dozens of events and the biggest problems are threefold.

Firstly most people are there to sell and not to buy, second there is often no quality control over who is there and finally there may be many competitors.

This means you can spend vast amounts of time communicating with people just on the off chance you might bump into someone who is interested in what you have to sell.

Now, don't think for a minute that I am not an advocate of attending networking events. I am, but attendance must be with purpose. Later in this book I shall give you an opportunity to receive a toolkit on how to make the most of formal networking events. Tips that are designed to maximise the amount of time you spend with people who are worth talking to!

So that's the five biggest mistakes. If any of these problems apply to you then take some time out to think about your approach.

Three Things You MUST Do

Before I begin this part it is worth pointing out that networking is quite a natural thing to do. Day to day we don't realise we are networking until we are introduced to the word. Think about all the people you talk with to share ideas, solve problems, exchange contacts, sell your products & services and have a gossip & laugh with. It's all networking.

Putting it simply, human beings are social creatures. We cannot perform at our best if we are deprived of contact with other people. So all I will be doing in this book is helping you to do what comes naturally!

This chapter covers the three things you must do if you want to become a top networker plus a diagnostic to check how well you are currently performing. As I mentioned in module 1, at Bozeat Consulting we have had the good fortune to research many high performing networkers as well as many inexperienced people.

There is no guessing which there are more of!

The three things you must do to 'Work the Net' are:

- Know who you want to rub shoulders with
- Have something great to say
- Adopt a 'give first receive later' attitude

Let's cover these one by one

1)   Know who you want to rub shoulders with

A good friend of mine Andy Mouncey runs a business called the 'Coach Company'. He helps people 'Find their Sparkle' and bring more energy into their lives. To introduce people into his business, which specialises in motivation, health & fitness, Andy uses some amusing metaphors as part of his seminars & health clinics.

He asks a member of the audience to reach into a bag & pull out a present which they then unwrap. One of the presents is a Spice Girls video. He then asks the audience which is the Spice Girls most well known song. The answer is 'Wannabe' their first hit single with the memorable line…'Tell me what you want what you really, really want.'

Andy goes on to point out that like everything in life if you want something you need to have a clear idea of what it is. Of course this is blindingly obvious but from a networking point of view far too many people wander around hoping that they will bump into someone that they can do business with.

Top networkers are extremely focussed; they know who they want to meet by profession, job function and by name.

In my business we want to meet 6 types of people:

1. Senior executives &/or respected influencers in medium to large organisations who are looking to or struggling to accelerate the pace of change in order to meet business objectives.
2. Senior executives/partners in organisations who want their people to be able to become 'RainMakers' and win

bigger and better 'champagne' business' with higher net worth customers.

3. Senior managers/executives who realise there is a wealth of untapped potential in their workforce that is just waiting to explode into ever higher levels of contribution and performance.
4. Leaders of organisations dedicated to revitalising under privileged communities.
5. Well connected people who share our passion for networking.
6. Anyone who has a great relationship with any of the above!

It is crucial to spend time defining exactly what you want. However it is sufficient to realise that human beings are proven to be goal seeking organisms and that the clearer you are in defining specifically what you want the more likely you are you will get it!

Here is a simple 4 part exercise:

Write down 10 people you would like to build a strong relationship with. If you don't know their names, no matter, you'll find that out later; just use their position and company.

Now write down who you know now that might help you get to know that person.

As soon as you can arrange a meeting and ask that person for advice on how to get in touch.

Act on any good advice that you hear.

It may be that you will have to speak to other people and maybe do some research, however just this simple action will take you one step closer to the person & people you want to rub shoulders with.

As you take each step you'll expand your sphere of influence. All successful people have a very wide network. Ivan R Misner, perhaps the world's leading authority on Networking, states in his book 'Masters of Networking' that he can get any piece of information he wants with just three phone calls. Now that really is being connected!

2.   Have something great to say

You'll probably recognise the expression 'You'll never get a second chance to make a good first impression.' One of the skills I have spent many hours practicing is my personal advert. Something that will grab the attention of anyone I come into contact with. So when they ask what you do, your reply will cause them to ask something like 'that sounds interesting tell me more.'

One story that illustrates this comes from some individual coaching work we conducted in recent years with Jez Hyland. Jez is a highly accomplished Financial Services professional. One area we've coached him in is how to network with high net worth people.

This is part of his story:

"One weekend I had managed to arrange a game of golf with an extremely wealthy landowner. I had his undivided attention for several hours. As we walked down a fairway he asked me *'so what do you do?'* and in reply I gave the most weak, uninspiring and truly gutless reply ever. Something like *'I'm a self employed financial adviser.*

'Oh' came the response and we carried on playing not sharing one further word about business for the rest of the day. What a wasted opportunity!"

Jez & I then went on to work on what I call a '30 second elevator speech' This is a short mini-advert that describes succinctly who you are, what you sell, who you sell it to & typically what added value you bring to you clients.

Take a second and think about some of the most memorable TV adverts you have seen. They all work on the same principle. The A.I.D.A. formula. Grab the viewers ATTENTION in order to stimulate INTEREST that creates the DESIRE for them to take ACTION.

In the networking context the action is causing the person you have just met to want to know more about you and what you do.

Remember if someone doesn't already know you, at the first meeting to them you are the product or service. Studies indicate that people form a first impression within 11 seconds of meeting someone and their perception will last so work on it!

Here is a valuable tip. In your 30 second speech try not to give away anything that will cause the receiver to form an impression of what you do. For example, If you say "I'm an accountant" they will instantly form a picture in their mind of what they think an accountant is and does which, 99 times out of 100, will bear absolutely no relation to what you actually do.

I will give you my own example, if I believe I am talking to someone who might be interested in one-to-one business performance coaching my routine will go something like this:

"So what do you do Simon?"

(I reach into my pocket and hold out a handful of diamonds, sadly only artificial)

"I am a 30-minute business coach; I polish your organisations diamonds'

(This normally causes a pause and a curious look)

"Oh, that's different, what does that mean?"

"Let me paint you a picture by using an analogy"

"Have you ever worked with a personal fitness trainer?"

They answer yes or no

"Tell me from your experience or imagination what you think are the qualities of great personal fitness coach"

They list some.

You add your own list if they haven't said what you want adding:

"A great coach will:

Stretch you and get you to do things that take you out of yourcomfort zone

Inspire you to do the important things that you know you should do but havenot got round to doing

Challenge your excuses for not following through

Provide a source of support when the going gets a little tough

Do anything they can to help you deliver results and do it quickly"

I then add:

"Ultimately when you have worked with a great fitness coach for a while you will know that you could not have achieved exceptional results without their knowledge, inspiration and encouragement."

I follow up with the following statement:

"A 30-minute coach does exactly the same in business. Research and practical experience tells us that most people in business tap into a minor fraction of their talent and potential. We either coach managers to bring the best out of their people or sales and account management professionals to sharpen their saw when it comes to the second most important business skill. This is the ability to make an impact and persuade and influence powerful people to do what you want them to do.

We work one-on-one and with small teams where we guarantee outstanding commercial results."

This approach is 3,000% better than replying *"I'm a management consultant!"*

A simple exercise for you is to fix up a 20 minute meeting with a friend or colleague whose advice you respect and value. Ask them to pretend you've just met and to ask you what you do. You then reply with your elevator speech. Then ask for feedback from your partner on how well you passed the A.I.D.A. test and be prepared for some brutal feedback!'

I cannot stress enough the importance of having this advert. It's taken me about 2 months to get to the point where I can trip off in around 30 seconds just enough to get what I want across.

My acid test having delivered my elevator speech is to gauge whether they are interested in knowing more. This enables me to open up the qualification process by asking some questions and hopefully steer the conversation towards setting up a formal meeting.

3   Adopt a 'give first receive later' attitude

In the U.S. there is a highly respected motivational speaker called Zig Ziglar, sadly he is no longer with us. He was one of the best speakers on the circuit. He delivered exceptionally powerful talks to audiences the world over. I remember one phrase he uses. *'You'll get everything you want in life if you'll help enough other people get what they want.'*

Parents often talk about Christmas being a time for giving rather than receiving, although I'm not sure all kids get the message! Another belief people have is *'what goes around comes around.'*

Also anyone who is successful in business will tell you the importance of delivering exceptional customer service. There is a very successful referral organisation called B.N.I. which advocates a philosophy of 'givers gain' all of this points to one universal truth, the more you give out the more you will receive.

Many inexperienced networkers when they meet a prospect fail to find out what the person wants and, if she is in the sales profession, what type of person they would like to do business with.

This, quite frankly is a big mistake.

Top networkers become a hub for people to meet each other. As your sphere of influence grows then the easier it is to connect people. If you are perceived as someone who knows a lot of influential people and is more than willing to refer people to each other then you become what I call a 'business hub.'

You'll be amazed at the number of influential people you'll naturally attract which makes networking that much easier!

Adopting this approach is largely a matter of ATTITUDE. In my experience most people are very guarded about referring others.

This is a missed business opportunity. As we shall see in later chapters providing personal introductions (PIs) can be extremely lucrative!

Here are a few tips about how to adopt a 'give first receive second' attitude.

When you meet someone who wears a sales hat ask them who an ideal client would be. This simple question will reveal specifically the type of person they would like to be put in touch with. Note that we are not talking about you selling them here, we are talking about you helping them to get what they want.

Take time to listen to people's needs and wants. Everyone has problems that need solving. Keeping a good track of who wants what will allow you to connect people and become a 'business hub'.

Be wary of who you refer to others. The best way to gauge how good someone in their organisation is through direct experience otherwise you will need to rely on their reputation by listening to what others have to say.

Get into the habit of collecting business cards of people who you respect and whatever you do keep in touch!

I've put together a quick diagnostic so you can assess how well you are currently 'Working the Net'. This is in the form of 10 statements. For each statement give yourself the following rating:

✓ Always	=	5 points
✓ Most of the time	=	4 points
✓ Sometimes	=	3 points
✓ Occasionally	=	2 points
✓ Never	=	1 point

1. When I meet someone who I believe may be well connected I take the time to understand what they do and who they might be interested in connecting with.
2. I have an excellent record keeping system that keeps track of what influential people want that I may not be able to provide.
3. I put people in touch with each other and act as a 'business hub.'
4. I keep in touch regularly with people who matter to me.
5. It is easy for me to approach new people that I would like to build a relationship with.
6. I am always looking for opportunities to network with influential people.
7. My network is growing.
8. I deliver a powerful 15 to 30 second 'elevator speech' at every appropriate opportunity I get.
9. I am always well prepared before I attend a formal or informal networking event.
10. I am always to looking to learn more effective ways of rubbing shoulders with the people I want to do business with.

When you have completed this, take time to review all those you have marked less than 5 and consider what you are going to do about it!

It's action that counts!

Three Ways to Motivate Advocates

Just for a moment think about the easiest and best way to get business, naturally it has to be by personal introductions. In other words positive word-of-mouth advertising.

When you're building a business from scratch there is no reason for anyone to refer you but as your reputation grows then so does the opportunity for personal introductions. However top networkers don't leave this to chance.

There is a distinct difference between those who network and those that 'work the net.' People who work the net are proactive and act with purpose. They have a systematic approach to expanding their network by creating the conditions which cause people to refer them to their colleagues.

Think about your business. How fabulous would it be if you managed to create an ever expanding group of influential advocates? It may be of course that you're doing that right now, if so well done!

It may be, however, that you wish to accelerate this process so more and more people are saying the right things about you, your company and your products or services. If so then this book is right for you!

In this chapter I am going to cover three ways of motivating people to become your advocates and point you towards other sources of terrific ideas to help you rub shoulders with the people you want to do business with.

1. Ask for personal introductions
2. Give them something they want & do it for free
3. Give them an incentive

Let's go through them

1 Ask for personal introductions

A short story. In 2001 we conducted some work with a company we'd been courting for around 2 years. They are a mid-size manufacturing company who were struggling to embrace the principles and practices of lean manufacturing.

Unfortunately some of the powerful people in the business were resisting the approaches of the 'pioneers' who wish to lead the company and its people into an exciting new era.

The MD had reached the point where external assistance and support was required to persuade them to change their ways. A project that was right up our street.

At a planning meeting with the MD we had concluded our discussions about the way forward. As I was about to depart I politely enquired about whether he knew of any other people who might benefit from the services we provide?

After a few seconds several names came to his mind who just happened to be people I've wanted to be introduced to but hadn't been sufficiently impressed by our direct mail campaign. He then promised to tell them not only about who I was but also to ask them if they were experiencing any of the problems I was going to be helping his company address.

32

What a result!

The key here simply is to ask. Naturally it is crucial that the potential advocate has some idea about who you are and what you and your company are capable of. Of course if they have had a favourable direct experience of your products and services then so much the better.

See if you can figure out which of these questions is most likely to get you the response you are looking for:

"Do you know of anyone who would be interested in learning about what we do?"

"Who do you know who would be interested in learning about what we do?"

2) Give them something they want for free

People remember the times when people do something for them that:

Has not been requested

Addresses a problem or fulfills a need they have

Is given for free

Everybody wants something for nothing, it's simply human nature.

As we operate in the service sector people buy information, ideas and advice from my company. The things we can supply for free are reports, tip sheets, advice on where to go to find the information they want, short periods of free consultancy, free seminars and contacts with other people.

An example of what we provide is this book. To prospective clients we give it away free, It is easy to give away and most people get a lot from it. It has something for everyone since everyone who wants to succeed in business has to network.

The best things to give away are those that you know the person wants which of course means you need to find that out directly or indirectly.

Beware of falling into the trap of ordering 1,000 cheap pens or badges with your logo on them & expecting influential people to be enthralled when they receive them. They are useful to keep your name in people's consciousness but not nearly as powerful as demonstrating you've put some effort and thought into who they are and what they want.

I love the part in the fabulous film 'Wall Street' when Charlie Sheen finally gets to meet Gordon Ghecko, (played by Michael Douglas) the obscenely wealthy businessman who he's pursued for months and months. In his first meeting he gives him a box of his favourite cigars.

It was this bit of research and a great deal of persistence that got his foot through the door.

Of course I am not advocating what he then did later in the film where he gets involved with insider trading and then gets caught & sent to jail, but it does make a cracking story!

A short exercise:

Write down the names of 5 people you would like to rub shoulders with.

Find out through whatever resources you have what they want and what turns them on & off. (You don't want to make a mistake and turn them off before you're even met them!).

Think about what you could give or send them that they would value which will not break your bank balance.

Send it with your compliments.

Get into the habit of doing this regularly with the people who you want like to rub shoulders with.

3 Give them an incentive

A quick question for you. What is the difference between a lead and a personal introduction (PI)? (We think PI is more endearing term than referral which is a little worn)

A PI is something you receive from a colleague that introduces you to someone who you know is in the market for the products or services you are equipped to offer. A lead is anything else. A PI is therefore more powerful than a lead and more likely to result in some business.

Here are three simple tips to incentivise people to give you PIs.

First make it financially rewarding. I have signed several 'introducers agreements' with business professionals who are both competitors and non-competitors. Quite simply for any

PI I give that leads to these organisations closing some business I will receive a percentage of the commission.

In my own business people who refer me can earn anything from 5% to 20% commission dependent upon the amount of sales effort we need to put in. Since people generally like money then finding a formula for giving people commission for PIs must be a good thing!

By the way if you too would like to earn some commission please give us a call.

Second, business people love to trade, but instead of money in exchange for a product or service, why not simply trade contacts. Every time you refer someone to a client make sure you get one in return.

Be careful to keep the numbers and quality of referrals balanced. No one likes to receive a dud. Too many of these will cause one side to call foul & the relationship to eventually collapse.

Third, if you ever get into a negotiation with a client who is not willing to pay you what you think you are worth then offer to reduce your price in return for a letter of recommendation to three of his customers plus an introduction. Ultimately that may deliver far more return than the money you had to give away.

Preparing For a Networking Event

In this chapter I'm going to help you learn how to prepare for a formal networking event.

At the time I found myself writing this chapter, we have entered my favourite time of the year, Spring. The season for a seemingly endless stream of B-B-Q's, barn dances, fetes and trips to country pubs. All terrific opportunities to get out and about.

It also might be that you are a fan of attending formal networking events. Organisations like the Business Links, Chambers of Commerce, Institute of Directors, BNI, Elite Entrepreneurs and many others are designed to bring like minded people together to make connections that will lead to business.

It maybe that you, like me, enjoy these formal and informal occasions as a chance to socialise and foster new, fresh and exciting relationships, after all networking should be fun!

There are many people, in my experience, who shy away from meeting new people. I find this a terrible shame not only because the potential for winning new business is enormous but people miss out on fulfilling a basic human need which is to connect with others.

One of the fundamental reasons why I think people shy away from making these connections is the lack of preparation.

Two short stories…

Some years ago I attended a formal networking event at Leicester Tigers Rugby Club. At the event were around 35 people from many different businesses. The event lasted around 2 hours during which we had a guest speaker, dinner and time to meet other people.

It just so happened that a sales representative of one of my newly acquired clients who I didn't know personally was there.

I couldn't help noticing that he only talked with one or two other people for the whole of the evening. I managed to eavesdrop on the conversation and noticed that everything other than business was being discussed. I could only imagine that as he drove away he thought the event was a total waste of time.

On the other hand I noticed many others walking away with a fist full of business cards with promises to meet up in the following days and weeks.

Again a few years ago I was waiting in the reception of a potential client's offices waiting to meet the Human Resources Director. Stood next to me in the waiting area was a Sales Director of one of their major suppliers who was, as I subsequently found out, waiting to see the Procurement Manager.

We struck up a conversation and as it turned out he was in the market for some training for his sales force, cards were exchanged with a promise to meet within a fortnight. Result!

These short examples illustrate the importance of making the most of formal networking events and also to be prepared at all times to take advantage of networking opportunities whether you are at a convention, dinner party, waiting in a queue, garden fete, 30,000 feet in the air or indeed just about anywhere!

In this chapter I'm going to cover three things you should do to prepare for a formal networking event:

- Find out who is going to be there and do some research
- Have your 30 second 'elevator speech' prepared
- Take your networking toolkit with you

One by one then...

1   Find out who is going to be there and do some research

This is the crucial first step, which surprisingly few people take. Top sales people recognise the need to do some background research on any potential client. There are four main reasons why you should do this.

First you can frame your introduction, questions and presentation to match the background and issues the client may be facing. Second it also shows you've done your homework which immediately raises your credibility and sets you apart from the rest. Third it ensures that the event itself is worth attending! Why waste your time travelling to a function where there is little chance of making any worthwhile connections?

Finally and most important it helps you focus so you spend more of your precious time at the event connecting with the right people.

2   Have your 30 second 'elevator speech' prepared

You will by now have realised the importance of the elevator speech. So you might ask why I have repeated it here. Simply because it's that important!

As part of the research for this book I interviewed one of the top producers in the Financial Services industry. In the past three years he's quadrupled his annual turnover, every quarter his income is greater than the one before and he only deals with people who have over £1,000,000 to invest!

Paul is a player by anyone's standards who continues to buck the trend in one of the toughest markets around. Now, all of his business is referred, so lead generation is very easy.

I asked him what he says to prospects when he first meets them. It will come as no surprise that it is vastly different from what the average Financial Advisor says. This to me indicates one thing; get very good at putting yourself across.

3   Take your networking toolkit with you

Some time ago my wife bought me a business card holder, it looks a little like a thin silver flip top cigarette lighter. At first I thought this was going a little over top until I began to use it and realised how useful it is.

First of all you can keep around 20 business cards in it, second it's a great place to store cards that you've received prior to adding to them to your sales contact system and finally it looks pretty groovy!

The card holder is just one non-essential item to add to your tooklit. However the following are essential:

Business cards, never ever be caught without one!

A diary to book the all-important follow up meeting

Some easy to read promotional literature that says just enough about who you are and what you sell

Some means of recording pertinent information that you learn about the prospect (I write mine on the back of their business card). A note pad (paper or electronic) is just as useful.

Working a Room

I'm sure you have been there either under your own steam or with your boss who has asked you to come along. Everyone has been to at least one networking event; a dinner, a chamber or business link bash, a sponsored event, a sales presentation, a party etc.

Whatever it is you will be in and amongst people you may have never met and you have a period of time to network.

In this part of the book we are going to look at five strategies for 'working a room.' If you've done your preparation thoroughly you will have already made a decision whether it is worthwhile going, you will have your 30 second elevator speech prepared and you will have your networking toolkit.

Ideally you will have already lined up colleagues, suppliers or customers who will introduce you to the people you want to do business with. If so well done! You have done most of the work now it is down to you to impress.

Have you ever noticed that at certain events there will be people that seem to attract other people around them? They seem to have an aura about them. Now, naturally if you are a Cameron Diaz, Andrew Flintoff (Go Freddy!) or Richard Branson, attracting people will not be an issue, however most of us do not have their record of achievement or looks. However all is not lost, there are a number of simple strategies and actions that will help you attract the people you want to be around you.

1. Be extraordinarily helpful to the organisers
2. Act as a host
3. Listen at least twice as much as you speak
4. Move!
5. Smile

One by one ...

1   Be extraordinarily helpful to the organisers

Anyone who has hosted an event will tell you how nerve wracking it can be especially when VIPs are present. It is always a good idea to bring the organisers on your side and of course a good way to do this would be to offer your services. Here are some things you can offer to do to help:

Make contact with important people who are due to come along to the event. The challenge most organisers of events have is getting the right bums on seats. Alternatively you can ask the organisers if it is OK to bring some important people with you.

Advertise the event through your own marketing channels.

Support them with logistics but be careful not to be drawn in too much as organising events can be very time consuming.

2   Act as a host

It is not uncommon during an event to notice people looking lost. Become good at drawing people into conversations.

People will welcome being drawn into discussions with people they would like to meet.

This is also a useful strategy as it allows you to gracefully disengage yourself from conversations with people that either have little to offer you or are a little tiresome. I am sure you know many people like this!

3 Listen at least twice as much as you speak

Five true stories that illustrate the point:

Some years back I met Thomas Wood. Tom is a top consultant and trainer in the US who conducts negations on behalf of private and public institutions. He told me this story:

He was due to attend an evening cocktail function with his wife and her work colleagues. On this particular evening Tom had just finished a two day seminar on negotiation skills to a group of senior clients.

In truth Tom had had a challenging two days and did not feel up to socialising. However he kept his promise to attend and assured himself that he would spend as little time as possible talking. True to his word Tom spent most of the party listening and occasionally chipping in with a comment or question.

As they were driving home at the end of the evening Tom received some feedback from his wife that many of her friends and colleagues thought he was by far and away the most attentive and interesting man at the party!

One of the happiest days in my life was the 15th September 1990 when I joined my wife Lynne in matrimony. It is a day I naturally remember well especially the sermon delivered by the Vicar once my wife and I had exchanged vows.

He described married life as a journey, a journey that will have many highs and inevitably some challenges that will test the strength of the relationship. He said that these are the times when it is most important for both the husband and the wife to put aside any unhelpful emotions such as anger or guilt and **genuinely listen to their partners' needs and feelings**.

He then addressed the congregation saying *"let's face it gentlemen we are not very good at listening are we?"* Just about every woman in the congregation nodded their head in agreement while just about all the men bowed their head effectively acknowledging their guilt!

More than a century ago, a young woman who had dined with both William Gladstone and Benjamin Disraeli explained why she preferred Disraeli: "When I dined with Mr. Gladstone I felt as though he was the smartest man in England. But when I dined with Mr. Disraeli, **I felt as though I was the smartest woman in England.**"

An American Ben Feldman was the first insurance salesman in the world to pass a sales goal of $25 million in just one year. He was asked about the secret of his success. His reply… **"Work hard, think big and listen well"**

Towards the end of the last century I had the opportunity to deliver a short seminar on the subject of listening to a group of 100 managers and senior professionals in a multi-national company. The talk was part of a two day conference. During my speech I delivered a 1 minute story in the most mundane, boring and uninspiring manner that I could muster. I then asked 10 questions to the audience about what they had just heard.

Most people scored less than 5 and only one participant scored a maximum 10. He did go on to say that he had learned from both his parents who are practicing and highly respected psychologists. This means that they were excellent at listening to people no matter how they put themselves across.

These five stories illustrate one inescapable truth, being able to listen is the most important communication skill and yet seemingly it is the most difficult for most of us to master. However the good news is that with some practice, patience and dedication anyone can become an accomplished listener.

Note: I will at this stage reveal that evidence exists that proves that women are generally better at listening than men!

"My wife says I never listen to her. At least I think that's what she said!"

Anonymous

I believe that listening is indeed the most important communication skill so I decided to give you some more material including 3 key listening skills. You will find these later in the book.

In addition we will help you uncover why so many people struggle to listen well, how to spot whether someone is not listening and the hallmarks of accomplished listeners.

4 Move!

Oh dear, how many times I have I observed people who are, quite frankly, poor at working a room. They only talk to people they already know and if they do meet someone they feel comfortable with they spend all their time with them. I've even seen people arrive with their colleagues from the same firm and spend all their time with them. That's not networking, it's socialising!

A useful strategy is to set a small goal of the number of business cards you would like to receive plus the number of meetings you would like to arrange as a result of attending the networking event.

5 Smile

Contrary to popular belief it doesn't take twice as many muscles to frown as it does to smile. Contact this amazing website for proof. http://www.straightdope.com/columns/040116.html

However, smiling does project warmth, you are never going to endear yourself to anyone unless you have an engaging presence about you so just smile!

How to Strike Up a Conversation

In this chapter you will learn 5 ways to initiate and make the most of a first conversation with someone you have never met before and seemingly may not have anything in common with.

A short story,

'Attending a meeting of the Food and Drink Forum on 7th February 2012'

In the previous decade or so I have had the good fortune to listen to, interview and work with many business leaders in prestigious firms representing the food industry. These have included Marstons, Everards, Molson Coors, SAB Miller and Samworth Brothers.

On this day the reason for my visit to the Forum was to meet and listen to leading experts in the industry and explore the possibility of putting on a major Food Industry related event in the Midlands. However there was another agenda.

In my world I am always looking to build relationships and partnerships with the most talented people in their field. Two reasons – they are terrific to listen to and learn from. Second working with talented, time poor and ambitious people is always a privilege and helps to pay the bills!

In any event I attend whether it is a one-to-one, small or large group I am always interested in who I can meet, what value I can offer and what others might be able to do for me and both my business and personal life.

To get the most out of these events the keys for me are:

- To genuinely have an open mind (few of us have this if we are really honest about it!)b
- Being prepared to initiate conversations
- To be curious about other people, after all we all have a unique story
- Listening really hard for glimpses of interesting information which I can build on
- Some kind of game plan; both who I'd like to meet and potentially form an ongoing relationship with
- A short list of things I can offer to others (in my case invitations to my events, connections with people in my network
- To help people open doors to the people they want to do business with)

On this occasion I thought that the guest speaker was going to be talking about a subject of which I had no interest. It turns out that I could not have been more wrong.

His chat about being made redundant and what it takes to secure a new position had something for everyone in the room.

After waiting for the appropriate time on AOB I delivered a well rehearsed opening pitch with a couple of free offers and subsequently was inundated with requests. One follow up e-mail the next day with my options for moving forward and all kinds of opportunities opened up. So why was this a successful 2 hour event for me?

- A good group to connect with
- No unhelpful thoughts before I visited the group

- Rehearsal and preparation
- Some good things (mostly complimentary) to give away
- Being proactive to offer first and receive second

As discussed earlier I am going to highlight five ways you can initiate and make the most of first encounters with people that initially you may have nothing in common with

Here they are...

- Be curious about meeting people 'cos you just never know...
- Listen really hard
- Ask great questions
- Be proactive
- Be grateful

One by one then...

1. Be become curious about meeting people 'cos you just never know...

I once had a coaching relationship with a wonderful and highly successful finance professional in a leading UK multi-national.

It is reasonable to suggest that Julie was more interested in numbers, spreadsheets and using her well
developed forensic skills to interpret reams of financial data in preference to learning networking skills!

Julie was ready to move up to the next level with aspirations to take on a leadership position in an operational role. Also with the advent of cost cutting within their clients the word had come down that building relationships at all levels with the customer base was critical.

Even with these twin pressures Julie was struggling to understand why working the Net and spending time learning relationship building skills was important.

My response was this 'Julie when you look back on your business life will you remember all the forms and spreadsheets you completed or will it be about the people you've met and spent time with?' Her response 'Good question' was enough.

I remember reading an article about Bill Clinton. Since his college days he'd kept a database of all the people he'd come across with notes about each person. Wow! Even after decades he would be able to look up and hook up with people. Now he is one of the most influential people on the planet who is most certainly curious about people!

Personally I am just always amazed at the wonderful things people disclose about themselves and how our lives are enriched by meeting good people.

During my training for a triathlon I was being trained by a rather gorgeous ex-competition swimmer who'd turned to coaching. In a rather surreal conversation with me in the water and Mandy on the poolside we exchanged notes about our respective professions.

She subsequently disclosed that since quitting competitive swimming years earlier she had never returned to the water.

When I suggested that I was writing a book about the psychology of getting in shape she was more than delighted to help out with my writing.

You just never know who you are going to meet and what might happen as a result...

2. Listen really hard

Listening really is the most important communication skill. It is the basis of all rapport, persuasion, influence and inspiring people to want what you want.

In all conversations there are always comments that indicate something deeper and interesting. Sometimes they are just throw away lines. An accomplished listener will quickly and appropriately pick these up and maybe build on them to initiate a fascinating and revealing dialogue.

When we teach people how to listen it is almost a revelation for the clients when they realise just how much wasted effort there is in just talking.

We don't have the time here to go into all the reasons why struggle to listen and then help you develop accomplished listening skills. However do use these lines next time you are in a conversation:

"So what you're saying is..."

"Can I just check that my understanding of what you're saying is right...?"

3. Ask great questions

The prelude to great listening is great questions.

In my profession questions are everything. Even this morning when I was writing this course my own business
coach Dr Rakesh Chopra was on a call with me. His first question was 'Where is your mind today?'

I have never been asked it before and it was a wonderfully incisive inquisition into some of my deepest thinking.

When meeting people for the very first time there will and should be some pleasantries to break the ice. Any innocuous subjects are useful; how you came to be there, people you both know, how's business, current items news/sport etc or even the travel and the weather.

Here are some of my favourite questions to initiate conversations:

> What brought you here?

> What are the biggest challenges you face in your business right now?

> I've heard about how well your business is performing, could you share with me the secrets of your success?

> Tell me about what has made you so successful?

> What could we chat about right now that make the best use of our time?

Tell me, if we were to look back at this conversation that we're about to have and considered it to be an extremely valuable use of our time what would we have talked about and what would have happened?

4. Be proactive

Why is it that two people can go to the same event and both have entirely different views and attitudes towards the experience? It's a little like people who go to a party and remark 'Well that was a waste of time' whilst others have a ball. Chances are that the latter are a little more proactive in making things happen.

Here are 5 ways to be proactive

1. Find out a little about the individuals, their business and the location before you arrive
2. Consider putting together an easy and simple agenda which you can use to get things going
3. Offer a gift to the person or people when you meet them. (I give away my booklets and they always go down well).
4. Think about a great question or two to start proceedings
5. Bring someone with you who you know the other people would love to meet – this always goes down well

Even if there is nothing immediately apparent where you can work together then don't worry. One of my favourite analogies is 'moulding the clay'. I have been in conversation with an associate for several years and we have yet to finalise something! Just one of those things, perhaps one day we will finish the clay and turn a lump into a masterpiece.

5. Be grateful

Sadly there will be many reading this who will not appreciate this. Their attitude will be 'I can't waste time talking to people who are no use to me, I've got a job of work to do'. For many, perhaps more enlightened people, the act of meeting and forming new relationships is a gift always to be treasured.

Often in business people do lose sight of the fact that it's not ALWAYS about the numbers and you never know who you might meet and what might happen as a result.

People are natural connectors and WE ALL need the nourishment that relationships bring. When accomplished leaders allow others to give them an insight into their world they consider it a privilege; do you?

Your Three Types of Network

A short story...

It truly is quite astonishing what happens when you decide to become a 'business hub'. You may remember from earlier that a 'business hub' takes the time to connect people together where one party has a need and the other the means & resources by which the need can be satisfied.

In doing so the business hub may draw some form of benefit, sometimes financial, but most of the time they do it because 'it's the right thing to do.'

A short time ago came across two influential businessmen at two separate networking events who just happened to be in the market for financial expertise. This is not a service we provide at Bozeat Consulting. However two short requests for help from my network via an e-mail produced an enormous response.

Any replies that suited the requirements of the potential client were forwarded on. The total time I personally invested in sending the message to the network & forwarding the replies was around 20 minutes spread over 2 weeks.

I'm not sure if any business came from this however I did receive a huge thank you from one of the prospects as I'd saved him both time & money. He did indicate that nobody had done anything like this for him before and that there was every likelihood that our paths would cross in the very near future.

He will shortly become the MD of a rapidly growing £19 million business and who knows, maybe one day, a valued customer!

They key question for you is, how regularly are you connecting people together?

In researching this programme I've read hundreds of books and articles and listened to countless audio tapes. Much of the research, I have to say, wasn't worth the effort however occasionally you come across some real gems. Here's one...

One piece of advice I've latched on to is the idea of designing and creating the network you want before you need it. The most important reason for this is utilisation of your time. Top performers cannot afford to waste any time & having a network of people you value & trust just makes life easy.

Stephen Covey in his fabulous book, The Seven Habits of Highly Effective People, talks about 'starting with the end in mind'. In the context of this book here are three questions you might like to consider...

- In an ideal world who would you want in your network?
- Who, ideally, would you most like to connect with?
- If there were three people in this world that you would like
- To build a fabulous relationship with, who would they be?

Simply by answering these questions you will begin to envision your perfect network which will, of course, lead you consider the relationships you wish to cultivate.

The ultimate goal of this book is to help you rub shoulders with the people you want to do business with. However there are three types of network that you must develop if you are to lead a healthy, balanced & prosperous business & personal life.

Your Support Network

A network of people that provide you with emotional and practical support. These may be family members, friends, local community groups and neighbours.

Your Information Network

To be successful in any occupation you need quality information & lots of it. People in the information network consistently provide you with knowledge to help you solve problems and meet the challenges that all leaders in business face.

Your Referral Network

A source of high quality leads from informed, respected and reliable people.

Try the following two-part exercise.

Part 1

Think of and write down three valuable pieces of information that you would like to have that would require some effort to obtain and as far as you know aren't available on the open market. Each of the three pieces of information must make a significant difference to the prosperity of your business if you had it in your possession.

Now consider how long it would take you or someone who works for you to get them. Think about whether the time & effort would be shortened considerably if you had cultivated better relationships in your network.

Part 2

Write down the last ten pieces of major business you delivered where the initial lead was generated from a referral. Now consider whether the current frequency and quality of the referrals are sufficient to develop the business at a pace that matches your aspirations.

On the 'How to Build a Profitable Business Network training programme we spend a short time discussing all the skills & resources you need to access to run your life effectively and where you might source them from. The participants are often surprised when they realise just how few people they know and can rely on for support, information and referrals.

If you, like most people, have gaping holes in your network then beware the possibility of having to waste vast amounts of your time searching for new and therefore potentially untested sources of support, information and referrals.

Knowing your network

"I find it difficult making connections..."

A lady once complained to me that she found it difficult to make connections with people and build up a network.

This was the essence of my reply:

'If you find it difficult to connect with people and you are in the business of selling then consider these two facts:

First, everyone needs something and everyone knows that to satisfy a need they normally have to trade something in return, usually money.

Second, people need a reason to connect with others, in the business world if people are going to invest time connecting with others they have to able to answer the question 'What's In It For Me (WIIFM)?'

Therefore, you must approach networking with the attitude of 'what can I do for this person that will help them get what they want?' once you've found out what it is you then help them get it!

If you then invest time building up a network of talented professionals, who you are willing to connect with others, you can easily get yourself into a position where you can help to satisfy just about anyone's needs.

Dependent upon how well you organise the network, where you receive something in return for passing on referrals, you can make yourself extremely wealthy in the process. Now that is worth thinking about!'

Note: I did think that if she wasn't prepared to learn how to connect with people her sales career would be fairly short!

A short story…

'The power of persistence, doing a good job and making it known that you are an active Networker'.

In early Spring 2003 we delivered a taster seminar for the Institute of Directors called *Breakthrough!* This is one of our core training programmes designed to help people rediscover their hidden potential. One of the delegates, as I subsequently found out, was a successful entrepreneur who had built up a business as a sub contractor to the likes of Ford, Honda, Peugeot, Land Rover and Bentley.

After around 10 phone calls and a couple of meetings I was asked to deliver a short seminar using the Breakthrough! methodologies to his entire team. None of them had ever been on a seminar anything like *Breakthrough!* And fortunately it was extremely well received; so much so that we went on to deliver a series of short seminars to increase the overall professionalism of his team.

The client was well aware of my interest in networking but refused to attend 'The Accomplished Networker' because he's got more work than he can possibly handle! Plus he was already exceptionally well connected given his status as an expert in his field.

With this in mind he was very keen to introduce my business to his key contacts in the aforementioned companies as well as developing a series of high quality training 'Master Classes.'

He also asked me to look into sourcing some other services, which just so happen to be in my contact book.

Yet another example of why it is so important to 'Work the Net!'

In this chapter I will give you 1 of over 25 planning tools provided to participants on the

How to Build a Profitable Business Network training programme plus a quiz that tests your knowledge of the people in your network. I guarantee you will be very surprised by how much you don't know!

Previously we covered the three types of network: Support, Information & Referral. During the training programme we encourage the participants to write down everyone they already know in each of these three networks.

The following statements give an indication of where to find sources of support...

- Your mentors or coaches
- People you have taught, coached or mentored
- People you have helped
- Your colleagues & friends from school/college/university
- Your family & close friends
- Other members of non-business groups
- Your former bosses & teachers

Why not take some time to write them down now. You'll soon find many sources of support that have lain dormant and are just ready to be reactivated!

And now a quiz, WARNING! Be prepared to not know the answers to some of these questions!

You will agree that if you want to build a relationship with someone it is important to know a lot about who they are, what they have done, what they do now and what they intend to do in the future. It is also important to understand something personal about the individual.

Try this exercise with three people in your network who you consider it essential to have an excellent relationship with. Score yourself 4 points for a complete answer & 2 for a partial answer.

- Nickname
- Date and Place of Birth
- A favourite colour or food
- Best friend (other than yourself)
- Mentor/sponsor/role model/hero (other than yourself)
- Favourite TV program/song/hobby
- A personal &/or business award/recognition
- Job title and at least one major responsibility
- Name and title of current boss & at least one colleague
- Major business issue/objective/problem
- Name and location of another company he or she has worked for

- Career objective(s)
- Key features and benefits of his or her product/service
- One or more of the community groups, clubs or organisations he or she has belonged to, office or position held, and name of at least one other member
- One or more business associations he or she has belonged to, office or position held, and name of at least one other member
- Name of at least one educational institution attended
- Names of publications he/she reads on a regular basis
- Family details, home address, telephone, partners name, number and names of siblings, dates of birthdays

The maximum number of points you can score is 72, most people score less than half and often that is about somebody they supposedly know extremely well!

Frightening isn't it!

Becoming a 'Revenue Enhancer'

All my feedback from this book points to one fact, people who are reading and acting on the tips and skills described are reaping the rewards. If you are reading this and you haven't taken action, why not? What could possibly be preventing you from adopting some of the easy habits described in this publication?

Maybe so far you haven't been inspired sufficiently to apply some of the techniques. If this is the case then I might have a simple 5 - step process just for you. Do this & I guarantee new opportunities will surface as if by magic!

In researching this book I came across an interesting new term, becoming a 'Revenue Enhancer.' This caught my attention until I realised it's an American phrase for someone who, in my parlance, 'Works the Net.' However, in straightforward terms, it means making money for your clients as well as for yourself.

So, how do you do it? And more importantly, why would you bother? The 'why' is very clear, client revenue enhancement will enable you to stand out from all your competitors and create far greater loyalty than any price cut or special deal ever will.

Today, even in one of the toughest trading conditions we have experienced in recent years you don't have to be the cheapest. In fact you can charge more for your services, because you are in fact giving more.

You are giving referrals to your clients at no extra charge, as well as providing your normal exceptional service. The 'how' is also relatively easy and may just require a little lateral thinking on your part. We all know that the key to business growth is getting customers to buy twice and in fact turning them into a client and ultimately an advocate.

Step 1

Look at your client base-be it 10 clients or 1000 clients-and, if you haven't already done so, grade them into A, B and C clients depending on the frequency or volume of orders or whatever your criteria may be. By doing this you will clarify where your business is coming from and what can be done to ensure that you do not lose even one of our major accounts.

Now choose to work from the top client right through to the bottom. People often make the mistake of dismissing small clients, not realising that they may just be one of a number of service providers for that company. But if they were to gain a greater market share of their business, they could become one of their major accounts.

Step 2

One by one, look at these clients and ask these 2 questions:

- How well do you really understand their business (not yours)
- Do you have any idea of the sorts of customers they are looking to do business with?

The clearer you are on this one point, the easier the revenue enhancement becomes. If you're unclear, why not phone your key person and ask the specific question: "Describe to me the perfect customer for you".

You may choose to explain that this is part of your client retention program this year will be your intention to refer business to this client.

Don't be surprised if they are taken aback with your offer. Record their responses.

Step 3

Start asking yourself these 2 questions:

- Do I know anyone who fits this description?

- Do I know anyone who knows anyone who fits this description?

Maybe you don't know anyone today; however, you now know what you are looking for. Repeat this process for maybe 10 clients at a time.

Without doubt, you will find that you already know people who are potential prospects either in your client base or your associates.

Step 4

Now it is a simple case of connecting two people together. When you do make the initial call, ask the client to send you five of their business cards. When they ask why, explain that this will make it a lot easier for you to refer business to them, if you can just give their business card to the potential prospect. You then create a specific referral business card holder, that would be portable, as well as an electronic record.

Step 5

Most importantly, before you place their business card in your referral holder, write your name on the back of their card- 'referred by Norman Smith'. You may decide to work on giving referrals to just ten clients per month and another ten the following month.

Energy follows thought. What we think about in our lives, is what we create for ourselves. If our intention is to give referrals to our clients, we will find that this happens. Basically, it's as simple as having their business card available and giving it to a prospect at an appropriate time.

Linking people with similar interests, potential business objectives and opportunities is great fun and very satisfying. The by-product will be more business and referrals for you and all it took was a little of your time and a little lateral thinking. And, always remember-what you give out comes back ten fold!

Are You Listening?

I have a friend and neighbour who is an absolute delight to spend time with but has an irritating habit that used to bug the life out of me. During conversations she will, without warning, interrupt and either change the subject or ask a question that is normally unrelated to the current subject. Imagine how irritating that is!

Perhaps you know people like that, chances are you probably do. Fortunately now, when our friend does this, my wife and I pick her up on it and we have a good laugh. The fact is our friend is like many people, she has yet to master the art of listening.

A colleague recently asked me to put some words together on the importance of learning how to listen. This is for a project to train business advisors how to interview business owners who are struggling to keep their business afloat.

As we researched the programme I was reminded of the quote…

"God made us with two ears and one mouth & he intended us to use them in that proportion!"

Listening, for many people, is tough to do and as we know, both from experience and research. As we discussed earlier listening is the most important communication skill yet only a minority of people genuinely listen well.

Of course, listening is a crucial skill for the accomplished networker. The question for you in this book is how good are you at listening?

"The most basic of all human needs is the need to understand and be understood.

The best way to understand people is to listen to them"

Ralph Nichols

A recent survey was conducted with a range of executives from various different companies on the subject of recruitment. 73% of them considered listening an 'extremely important skill' yet when asked how many of their recent hires had 'good listening skills' their response was only 19%.

Listening is, of course not just for business, it is a life skill that, when applied well forms and strengthens all relationships. It is reasonable to suggest that listening is **the most important communication skill yet for many the most difficult to master.**

We will cover…

1. Why people struggle with listening
2. How you know somebody isn't listening
3. The benefits and hallmarks of an **Accomplished Listener**

Why is it that people struggle to listen?

- There are many reasons why people find it tough to listen. For example:
- The speaker may not be interesting to listen to
- The listener may be experiencing unhelpful emotions which prevent him focusing his full attention on the speaker
- There may be environmental factors interfering e.g. noise or an uncomfortable climate
- There may be relationship issues which cause the people concerned to lack the motivation to listen
- Fatigue
- The listener believes that the only way he put their point across is to talk more and increase the volume!
- The listener lacks the ability to concentrate
- The listener cannot let go of a specific point and spends most of their time thinking about what they want to say rather than listen to the speaker

It is quite easy to spot people, who are incapable and/or unwilling to listen, they…

- Interrupt the speaker
- Finish the other persons' sentences
- More often than not start their response with "I hear what you are saying but…"
- Send all manner of non-verbal signals that indicate that they are not listening e.g. failing to make eye contact and fidgeting
- Love the sound of their own voice and talk too much

- Are judgemental
- Change the course of the conversation by responding with questions and comments that are unrelated the subject currently under discussion
- Give unsolicited and/or unwanted advice
- Have a closed mind and are unreceptive to other peoples' opinions and beliefs
- Give the impression that they are too busy and impatient to listen

Like most people who read these lists I'm sure you are thinking 'I know people like that'. The question is, do you know a person like that intimately?! Like maybe you!

People who exhibit these traits are missing out on so much, the opportunity to learn about and from other people. Only when we exhibit a sense of curiosity and fascination for what others have to say do we truly enrich our lives

"The older I grow the more I listen to people who don't talk much"

Germain G Glein

The hallmarks and benefits of becoming an Accomplished Listener

Good listeners…

- Pay attention to the context as well as the content the discussion. They are able to decipher the true meaning of both the words and what lies behind them
- demonstrate to the speaker that they are listening using non-verbal cues especially an appropriate amount of eye-contact
- are quick to establish rapport so others feel it is safe and secure to talk
- Regularly paraphrase the speaker without changing the meaning of what the speaker has said. (Someone who just hears and merely repeats the speakers' words is simply a parrot!)
- Steer conversations towards other peoples' interests. By doing this they switch from transmitting to receiving and in doing do opens themselves up to listening and learning
- Are sensitive not only the words being spoken but also the manner in which they are conveyed both in the voice and the physiology (body language). Often these will convey the true meaning of the words being spoken
- asks appropriate and meaningful questions in a non-threatening manner in order to seek out and clarify information
- have tremendous patience always giving the impression that they have time for anyone and everyone
- have the ability to metaphorically step into the speakers' shoes and see the world from their perspective
- demonstrate genuine interest in the other person irrespective of any differences in age, gender, race, background or beliefs

- Suspend any judgment and enters each and every conversation with a sprit of genuine curiosity. They resist (especially men) the temptation go into problem solving mode too soon

Good listeners are also great speakers; they learn how to be heard with the minimum of air time. They know that they have become an accomplished listener when they can utter two sentences in an hour-long conversation and receive thanks for the input from the other speaker who adds, quite earnestly... "You always have so much to say!"

Now we have established that learning how to listen is crucial we will cover just three straightforward listening skills.

Listening skill number 1: Take exceptional notes

I'm not sure about you but my memory could be a lot better. I remember listening to an interview with Richard Branson. He stated that one of his weaknesses is not remembering things. He does, however, carry a notebook with him at all times.

Listening skill number 2: Regularly clarify and summarise what you think the speaker has said

A question for you, how do you know that you have truly understood what another person has said? The answer is to test it out with them.

Get into the habit of regularly using these types of phrases…

"To check my understanding could I just summarise what we've covered so far ……"
"Just to make sure I understand you correctly……"
"Could I just clarify a couple of points……?"

A simple exercise I ask people to do when training is to find a partner who talks for a couple of minutes about a subject she knows a lot about. The other person is asked to ask questions to clarify any points he doesn't understand and at the end he must give an accurate summary of what she said. She then gives him marks out of 10 for accuracy.

Why not try this with a friend or colleague; you'll be amazed at how well you do.

Listening skill number 3: notice the speakers' response

"Feedback is the breakfast of champions"

These wise words were said by Ken Blanchard author of the best seller 'The One Minute Manager.'

All top performers search for feedback and are very self critical. Take the time to notice how the person you are talking to behaves and be very open and honest with your interpretation of their response.

Self awareness when learning anything is crucial. Here are a few questions you can ask yourself when listening during a networking conversation.

Are they warming to you?
Are they talking while you are listening?
Are you beginning to build a relationship?
Are your questions eliciting the response you want?
Are they happy to disclose information to you?
Are you using less air time than the speaker?
Are you maintaining focus and concentration?
Are you able to put any thoughts out of your mind that might cloud your ability to focus on what the speaker is saying?

"Listening is everything; it is how you learn everything"

Meryl Streep – Multiple Oscar winning actress

In the online 24/7 access training programme 'How to Build a Profitable Business Network' we introduce you to full ½ hour video to help you master listening skills using the proven P.E.C.A.N.S. approach

Summary

I trust by now you have applied some or all of the techniques in the book and are reaping the rewards. It also may be the case that you have read something and not done anything about it even though it made a great deal of sense. Shame on you!

However I know you are not one of the really sad people who buy a book then receive lots of valuable information which is stored in a file only to be read 'some day.' When that day comes they open up the file and notice how much there is. This puts them off and it finds its way into the archives never to be seen again. This can't be you because you have got this far!

In each of the modules we gave you stories, how-to's, how-not-to's, techniques and some secrets of people who have built exceptional networks of talented, influential and powerful people on their way to the top of their chosen profession.

We talked a little about the fact that most people are happy to learn a lot but the majority don't put into practice what they've been taught even though at the time it makes great sense.

A smart person once said…

"Everyone wants to be successful but not everyone wants to practice"

Everything you have read is the product of thousands of hours research through observation, personal experience and research. I hope that you are now better equipped to avoid making the mistakes that less experienced networkers make.

We covered why networking is so important and why it is an essential part of creating the conditions whereby your business is promoted through positive-word-of- mouth-advertising.

We covered the five most common mistakes made by inexperienced networkers.

We covered the three things you must do to 'Work the Net'

These are:

1)   Knowing specifically who you want to rub shoulders with

2)   Having something great to say

3)   Adopting a 'give first receive later' attitude

There was also a quick self-assessment diagnostic to help you assess where you are in relation to your networking activities and I hope you completed that.

Then we covered three ways you can motivate people to become advocates and help you rub shoulders with the people you want to do business with.

These are…

1)   Asking for referrals

2)   Giving them something they want & do it for free

3)   Giving them an incentive

Then we covered three things you should do to prepare for a formal networking event with your 'toolkit'.

Next came five simple skills and techniques for making the most of a formal or informal networking event.

Remember the idea of 'designing the perfect network before you need it.' It included the three types of network you need to be successful.

- Support Network
- Information Network
- Referral Network

Following that was just one of the 25 networking planning tools introduced to participants in our training programme. It covered where to go to obtain sources of support along with a quick quiz which demonstrates how little people generally know about the people in their network.

We then introduced the concept of a 'revenue enhancer' and a five step process for earning more revenue for your customers and you in the process.

Finally we worked on your listening skills - The most important skill of all in business networking.

That's not bad at all is it, lots of value for a very small outlay in the price of this book. If you take the time to learn these principles it will come back to you in spades.

Next Steps

It's been a pleasure having you keep with this course until the end.

BUT! It's not over yet.

I'd like to give you a free preview of my highly acclaimed video course "How to Build a Profitable Business Network. You can find out what I look like (scary experience) and take six short parts of the course for free.

Simply   visit www.simonbozeat.com/home/onlinevideotraining/newbpn/

Also see the online courses section of http://simonbozeat.com

About The Author

A graduate from Nottingham University Simon Bozeat first worked for The Ford Motor Company and later found himself in training and personal development subsequently holding senior positions in Lloyds, Siemens and GEC

During the 90's Simon worked with the best of the best in training. Companies such as Huthwaite Research, PE International and PTP training and marketing

Simon became an expert in Behaviour Analysis. He learned the behaviours that distinguish the top performers from the average, He also learned NLP via Tony Robbins

Simon found that executives, managers, sales and non-operations support staff often lacked one core skill, **the ability to persuade other people to want what they want.**

Consequently the first suite of Simon's training products became known as **'Persuading Powerful People'**.

In 1997 Simon launched his own business and his first major client was Rolls-Royce Aerospace based in Derby. The initial contract was for 6 months however it went on for 3.5 years. Simon is now a genuine authority on how to make colossal change happen.

Simon became know in Rolls Royce as 'Mr Facilitator'. Whenever a senior executive needed to bring people together to address challenging problems then Simon was called in as the man to make it happen. He is a world-class facilitator skilled in bringing people together with well-intentioned yet disparate thoughts to align them around a compelling vision of the future and route map to make it happen.

It was during this period that, without knowing it, he became a one-to-one business coach. With so much experience to draw on Simon can rapidly help talented, ambitious and time-poor business professionals address complex change and persuasion related challenges.

At the dawn of the new millennium Simon turned his attention to the professional services market and the sales challenges they faced. He spent 6 months interviewing many of the UK's leading law, accounting firms and banks. He asked one question: "What are the factors which contribute to and hinder sales success in your business?" The result is the acclaimed white paper. 'Making it Rain, how to skate anti-clockwise' and a host of opportunities followed training people to sell, persuade and influence

Towards the end of the first decade of the 21st century Simon spotted a gap in the market for high profile business clubs. He launched the Ashby Business Club in 2008 which morphed into the Midlands Leadership Experience (MLE) in 2010.

Simon took advantage of 2012, the incredible year of sport in the UK, to become a triathlete. He is currently writing a book about the experience called 'Tri'ing to get in shape, one lampost at a time' He is raising considerable funds for his nominated charities whilst training to increase his distances with an ambition to complete an Ironman triathlon.

Request

I really hope that you have enjoyed this book and find it useful.

If you have time can I ask that you do a little networking for me and give my book a positive review on the amazon book store?

Here are other ways you can help me.

Tweet that you have read this

Do a facebook post

Tell your friends

Thank you and I wish you...

Every Success!

Other Books by GD Publishing

Making It Rain by Simon Bozeat

http://bit.ly/makingitrain

21st Century Tactics by Glyn Williams

http://bit.ly/21stcenturytactics

The 7 Deadly Sins of Advertising By Glyn Williams

http://bit.ly/7-deadly

The Holy Grail Trading System By James Windsor

http://bit.ly/grailtrading

www.ingramcontent.com/pod-product-compliance
Lightning Source LLC
Chambersburg PA
CBHW071606170526
45166CB00003B/1016